Amazing Americans: Paul Revere

Jennifer Overend Prior, Ph.D.

Consultants

Shelley Scudder
Gifted Education Teacher
Broward County Schools

Caryn Williams, M.S.Ed.
Madison County Schools
Huntsville, AL

Publishing Credits

Conni Medina, M.A.Ed., *Managing Editor*
Lee Aucoin, *Creative Director*
Torrey Maloof, *Editor*
Marissa Rodriguez, *Designer*
Stephanie Reid, *Photo Editor*
Rachelle Cracchiolo, M.S.Ed., *Publisher*

Image Credits: Cover, pp. 1, 5, 6–7, 8, 9, 15, 19, 20–21, 24, 26, 32 The Granger Collection; p. 28 Joaquin Rodriguez; p. 3 The Library of Congress [LC-USZC4-2912]; p. 4 The Library of Congress [LC-USZ62-48901]; p. 12 The Library of Congress [001dq]; p. 12–13 The Library of Congress [LC-USZ62-50337]; p. 18 The Library of Congress [ar090000]; p. 22 The Library of Congress [LC-DIG-highsm-15388]; back cover, pp. 10, 14 (left & right), 16–17, 21, Nancy Carter/North Wind Picture Archives; p. 22 Preservation Massachusetts; p. 23 Stephanie Reid; All other images Shutterstock.

Teacher Created Materials
5301 Oceanus Drive
Huntington Beach, CA 92649-1030
http://www.tcmpub.com

ISBN 978-1-4333-7003-8

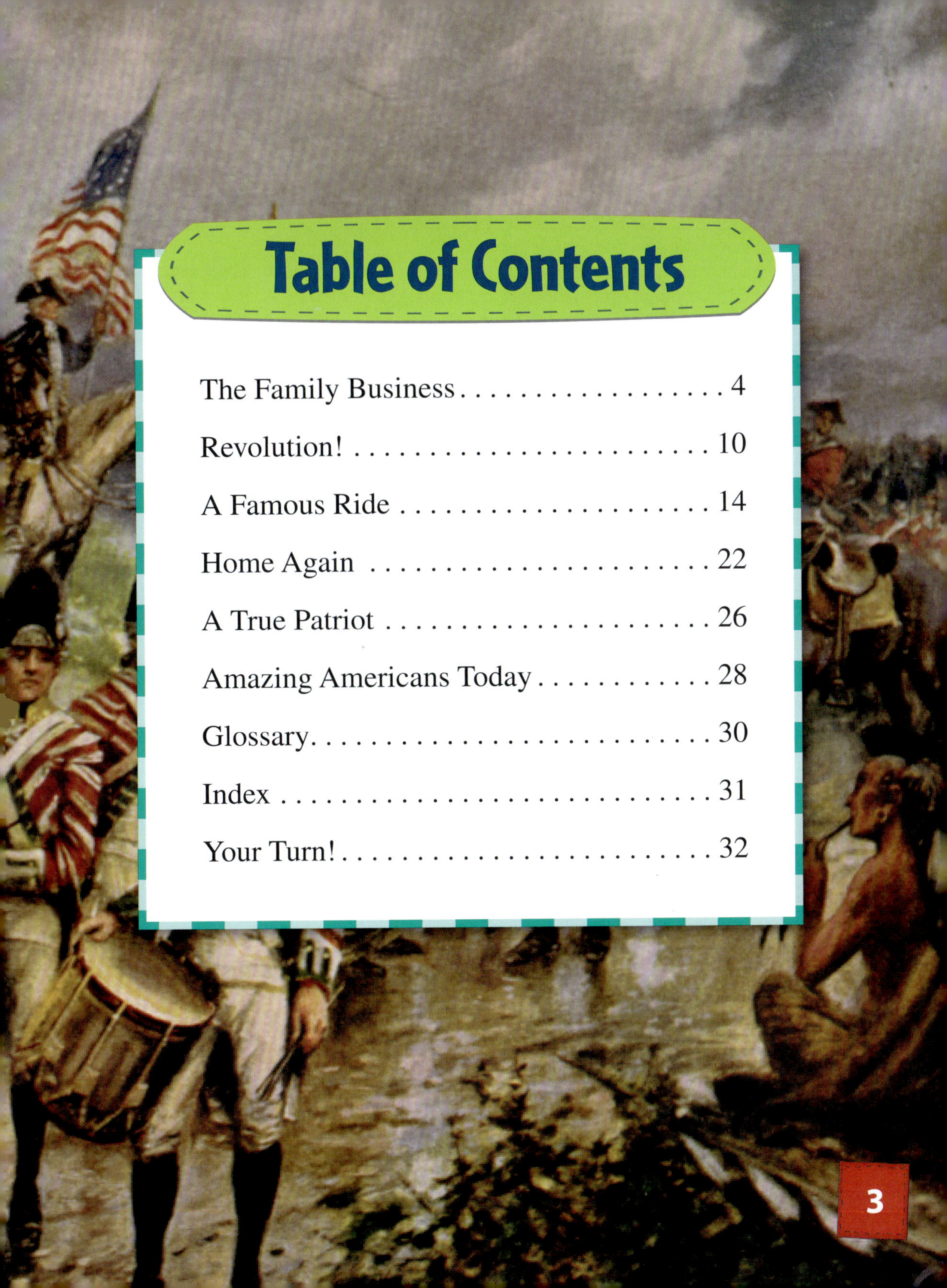

Table of Contents

This is the house where Paul was born.

The Family Business

Paul Revere was a man who loved his country. He was born in December 1734. Paul was the second of at least 9, maybe even 12 kids! No one knows for certain.

Paul Revere

The Revere family lived in Boston. Paul's father was a silversmith and a goldsmith. Paul was, too. They made things out of silver and gold.

Silversmiths and goldsmiths work hard. They pound metal into a shape. Or, they melt it and pour it into a **mold**. Then, it hardens into the shape of the mold.

These silversmiths are making things out of silver.

Silversmiths and goldsmiths make things people use. They make spoons, forks, and knives. They make cups and candleholders, too.

Tools of the Trade

Silversmiths and goldsmiths use many tools to make patterns and shapes in the metal.

These are silversmith and goldsmith tools.

Paul had many other jobs, too. He worked as a dentist and cleaned teeth. He also placed false, or fake, teeth into people's mouths. At that time, false teeth were only used for talking. People would take them out to eat food.

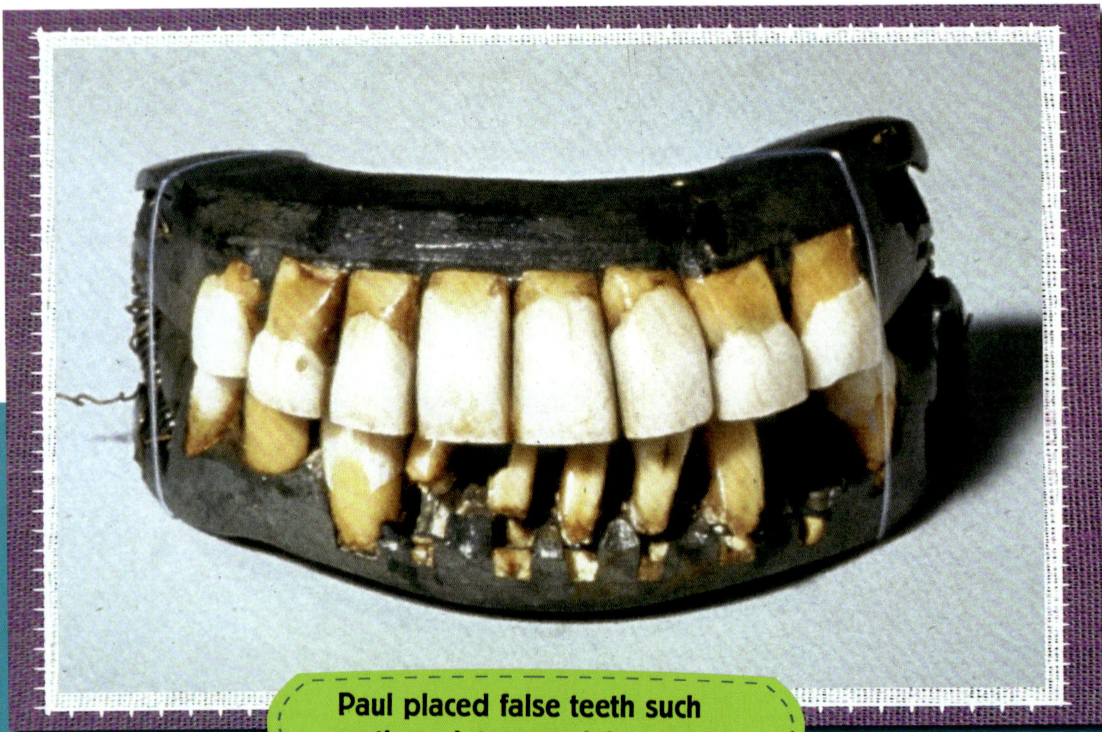

Paul placed false teeth such as these into people's mouths.

Paul was also an artist. He made pictures for books. He did this by carving pictures into metal. Then, the metal was used like a stamp.

This is one of Paul's pictures.

Revolution!

Paul lived in America before it was its own country. There were 13 **colonies** (KOL-uh-neez) ruled by King George of Great Britain. The people who lived in America were called **colonists** (KOL-uh-nists).

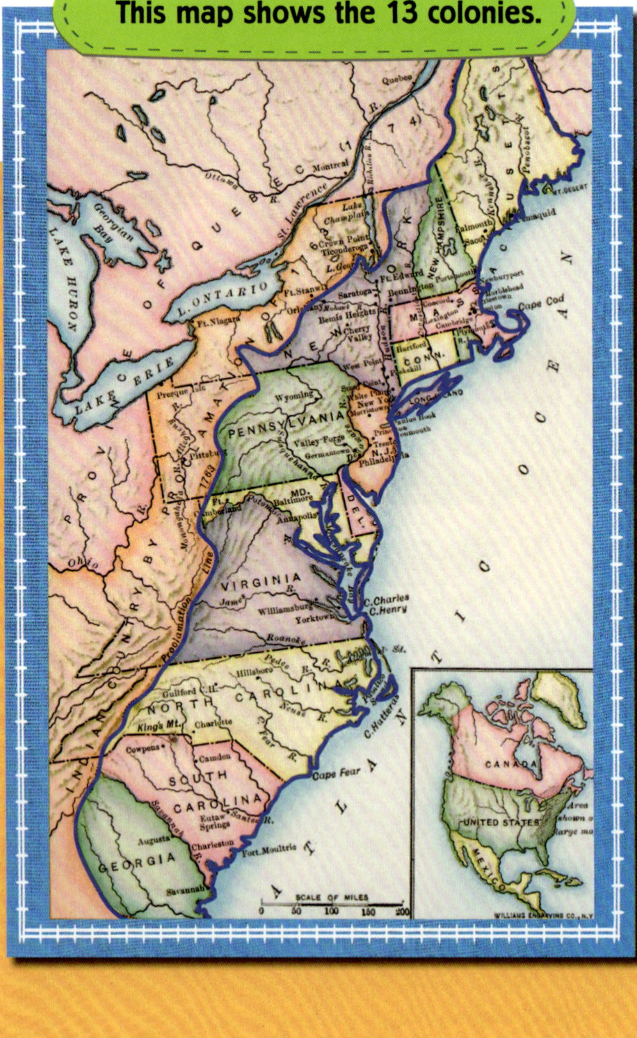

This map shows the 13 colonies.

The colonists thought the king was unfair. He did not let them make their own laws. The king wanted the colonists to pay higher taxes. They did not like the king telling them what to do.

Taxes

Taxes are money that people have to pay to the government (GUHV-ern-muhnt). The *government* is the group of leaders who make decisions for the country. The government uses the money to pay for things people need.

Colonists had to pay high taxes on things such as tea.

Colonists who wanted to be free from Great Britain were called **Patriots** (PEY-tree-uhtz). They wanted to start their own country. They held meetings. They made plans. Paul Revere was a Patriot.

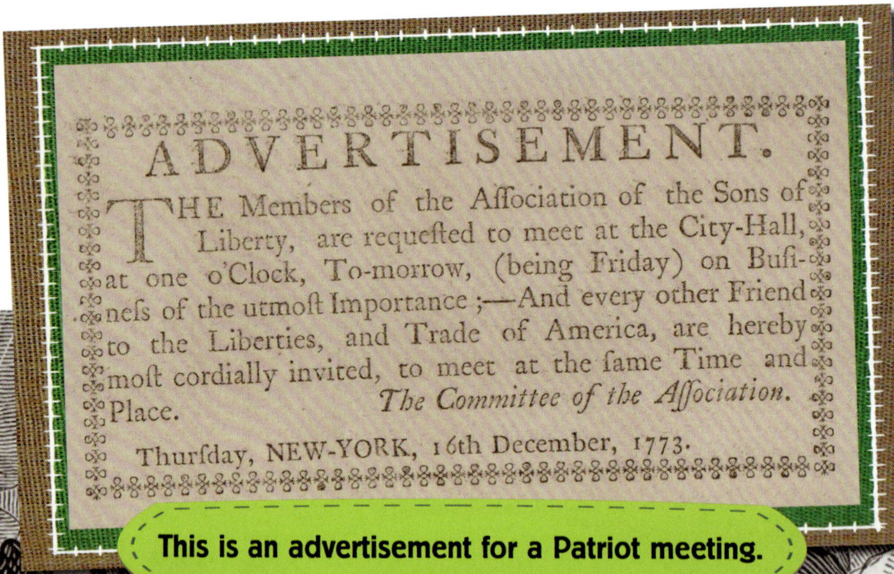

ADVERTISEMENT.

THE Members of the Aſſociation of the Sons of Liberty, are requeſted to meet at the City-Hall, at one o'Clock, To-morrow, (being Friday) on Buſineſs of the utmoſt Importance ;—And every other Friend to the Liberties, and Trade of America, are hereby moſt cordially invited, to meet at the ſame Time and Place.

The Committee of the Aſſociation.

Thurſday, NEW-YORK, 16th December, 1773.

This is an advertisement for a Patriot meeting.

The Patriots were not afraid to go to war. They were willing to fight for their freedom. They wanted their **independence** (in-di-PEN-duhns).

Sons of Liberty

Paul Revere was in a group called the Sons of Liberty. The group wanted the colonies to be free from Great Britain.

This is a Sons of Liberty meeting in 1773.

A Famous Ride

On April 18, 1775, Paul went to the town of Lexington. He had to warn two Patriots that the British were coming to get them.

Samuel Adams

John Hancock

Two Patriots

Samuel Adams and John Hancock were the two Patriots who Paul warned.

Paul asked a friend to hang lanterns from the top of a church. One lantern meant the British were coming by land. Two lanterns meant that they were coming by sea. Paul saw two lanterns.

This is one of the lanterns that Paul used.

What Did Paul Say?

Many people think that Paul yelled, "The British are coming!" He did not. But at one stop on his ride he did yell, "The regulars are coming out!"

Paul had two men row him across the river. Then he borrowed a horse from a friend. Paul rode to Lexington with another Patriot. His name was William Dawes.

Paul warns colonists that the British are coming.

Paul and William got to Lexington in time to warn the other Patriots. The colonists heard the warning.

Next, Paul and William left for Concord. They had to warn people to hide supplies that were there. They did not want the British to get them. Another Patriot named Samuel Prescott joined them in the ride.

This map shows Paul's path from Boston to Lexington.

The three men were soon **captured** by the British. Samuel escaped right away. He made it to Concord. William escaped next. Finally, Paul was released and went back to Lexington. The British kept Paul's horse.

Paul is captured by the British.

British soldiers march into battle.

On April 19, 1775, the British fought the colonists in Lexington. Then, they fought in Concord. These were the first two **battles** of the **American Revolution** (rev-uh-LOO-shuhn).

PAUL REVERE'S RIDE.

Listen, my children, and you shall hear
Of the midnight ride of Paul Revere,
On the eighteenth of April, in Seventy-five;
Hardly a man is now alive
Who remembers that famous day and year.

He said to his friend, "If the British march
By land or sea from the town to-night,
Hang a lantern aloft in the belfry arch
Of the North Church tower as a signal light,—
One, if by land, and two, if by sea;
And I on the opposite shore will be,
Ready to ride and spread the alarm
Through every Middlesex village and farm,
For the country folk to be up and to arm."

Then he said, "Good night!" and with muffled oar
Silently rowed to the Charlestown shore,

Then he climbed the tower of the Old North Church,
By the wooden stairs, with stealthy tread,
To the belfry-chamber overhead,
And startled the pigeons from their perch
On the somber rafters, that round him made
Masses and moving shapes of shade,—
By the trembling ladder, steep and tall,
To the highest window in the wall,

Where he paused to listen and look down
A moment on the roofs of the town,
And the moonlight flowing over all.

Beneath, in the churchyard, lay the dead,
In their night-encampment on the hill,
Wrapped in silence so deep and still
That he could hear, like a sentinel's tread,
The watchful night-wind, as it went
Creeping along from tent to tent,
And seeming to whisper, "All is well!"
A moment only he feels the spell
Of the place and the hour, and the secret dread
Of the lonely belfry and the dead;
For suddenly all his thoughts are bent
On a shadowy something far away,
Where the river widens to meet the bay,—
A line of black that bends and floats
On the rising tide, like a bridge of boats.

Meanwhile, impatient to mount and ride,
Booted and spurred, with a heavy stride
On the opposite shore walked Paul Revere.
Now he patted his horse's side,

This is a famous poem about Paul.

Famous Poem

A famous poem about Paul Revere begins this way: "Listen, my children and you shall hear/Of the midnight ride of Paul Revere."

Many battles followed. In 1781, the colonists won the war. America was free! It was now its own country called the United States of America.

Home Again

The war had ended. Paul went home. He opened a store where he sold tools. He also made church bells and parts for ships.

This is Paul's copper-rolling mill.

In 1801, he opened a **copper**-rolling mill. A *mill* is a building where something is made. Paul wanted to sell copper. This way Americans did not have to buy copper from Great Britain.

This man is rolling copper in a mill.

Paul had 16 kids. He had eight kids with his first wife, Sarah. She died years before his famous ride. Then, he married a woman named Rachel. They also had eight kids.

This is an ad for Paul's tool store.

Paul stopped working in 1811. He was 76 years old. He left his copper mill in the hands of his sons and grandsons.

Paul's sons continued to make copper bells like these.

A True Patriot

Paul Revere died on May 10, 1818. He was 83 years old. It had been 43 years since his famous ride.

Paul Revere

Paul Revere loved his country. He was a good **citizen** (SIT-uh-zuhn). He worked hard to help the Patriots.

This is a statue of Paul in Boston.

Amazing Americans Today

Paul Revere was an amazing American. He helped people by bringing them an important message.

Today, there are many amazing Americans. They help people, too.

This is Daniel with his sister Mayra. She helps people at the hospital in her free time.

Draw It!

Draw a picture of someone you think is an amazing American. Show what he or she does to help people.

Daniel drew this picture of Mayra.

Glossary

American Revolution—the American colonists' war for independence from Great Britain

battles—fights between people or groups in which each side tries to win

captured—to have caught someone by force

citizen—a member of a country or place

colonies—areas ruled by a country far away

colonists—people living in an area that is ruled by another country

copper—a reddish-brown metal

independence—freedom to make decisions

mold—a container into which liquids are poured and then harden to make them into a shape

Patriots—colonists who wanted to be free from Great Britain

Index

Your Turn!

Secret Message

This painting shows Paul Revere looking at the lanterns on top of the church. The lanterns sent a message.

Think of a special way of telling something to a friend. Then, send him or her a secret message.